CREATING SOLACE MOMENTS

21 Powerful Healing Affirmations
to Heal A Nation

TINA ALEXIS

Creating Solace Moments

21 Powerful Healing Affirmations to Heal A Nation

©2021 Tina Alexis

print ISBN: 978-1-09836-416-8
ebook ISBN: 978-1-09836-417-5

DEDICATION

This Book is dedicated to my dear family in Heaven. To my daughters, Ashley and Kennedy, you are the light in the darkness. Always allow your light to shine in the world.

To my nieces and nephews, you are the future. To all of the frontline workers, all of the young people who stood up and showed out for justice and change, you are all World Changers.

To the voters and protesters, who risked their health and lives during this COVID-19 Pandemic, thank you!

To all of the lives lost, we will always remember!

A WORD FROM THE AUTHOR

This book was created to induce healing, love, balance and peace. In the wake of COVID-19, social injustice, unfairness and racism, we need a healing! We need peace! We need love! Most of all, we need unity!

May this book bring forth blessings of peace, healing, forgiveness and most of all, positive change.

Be Beautifully Blessed!

~Tina Alexis

ABOUT THE AUTHOR

Tina Alexis is a phenomenal woman, who has overcome many challenges, great loss, tragedy and great adversity. Tina is a survivor of 9/11, has endured the painful loss of all of her immediate family, including her father and three brothers who died seven to eight months apart from each other, by which her father and 2 of her 3 brothers had cancer, the loss of her mother when Tina was at the tender age of twenty-one and a survivor of domestic abuse just to name a few. All of these experiences have led Tina to dedicate her life to uplifting, encouraging, enlightening and empowering the mind, life, spirit and heart of others.

In spite of all of these challenges, Tina has gone on to become a certified Community Leader, a Minister of Metaphysics, by which she holds a Bachelors in Metaphysics as well as a Certificate in Ministry. Tina also has her level 1 and level 2 certification in Reiki Energy healing and went on to the highest level of training to become a Certified Reiki Master. Although Tina wears many hats, the most important hat is being a mother and caring for her youngest daughter who is ten, living with Crohn's Disease.

Tina's inspirational work has landed her on local television and radio shows and magazine editorials, both domestically and internationally. Tina will always share her powerful message of inspiration, hope, faith and that the best in life is yet to come.

PRELUDE

It is said that it takes twenty-one days to break or change a habit, that is why I have created this book of twenty-one daily healing affirmations to help cleanse our minds and spirits of all of the negative, traumatic and painful experiences that this year has brought us. Simply read and repeat one of these powerful healing affirmations, daily, throughout the day. Anytime that you may find yourself feeling overwhelmed, anxious or doubtful, simply revisit these affirmations. I hope that this book restores hope, peace and balance in your heart, mind and spirit.

~ *"Today, I release the negative, traumatic and tragic experiences of 2020 and I allow my healing to begin."*

~ *"I am not the experiences that I have just gone through, and I look forward to a wonderfully hopeful new beginning."*

~ *"I am more than enough to accomplish anything, I am powerful, I am an overcomer!"*

~ *"I accept that my once normal way of life is now a new normal way of living."*

~ *"I accept my new reality and pledge to make life great moving forward!"*

~ *"I accept and embrace divine change in my life."*

~ *"Today, I celebrate all victories in my life, no matter how big or small."*

~ *"Today and every day, I release all negative feelings and emotions."*

~ *"Today, I embrace and welcome joy, peace and happiness into my life."*

~ *"Starting this very moment, I will strive to be the best human being that I can be."*

~ *"I will treat myself and others with value and respect."*

~ *"Today and every day, I will live my life in a state of love."*

~ *"Today and every day, I will practice the art of forgiveness."*

~ *"I welcome divine renewal, healing and restoration into my spirit."*

~ *"Today, I will respect the opinion of others, even if I disagree."*

~ *"I warmly embrace divine growth and change."*

~ *"I have the power to control my reactions to situations and others."*

~ *"I will not dwell in negativity."*

~ *"I choose to live life in love and not hate."*

~ *"I will not allow the negative actions and words of others define me."*

~ *"Today and every day, I embrace my divine self."*

3 STEPS THAT I WILL TAKE TOWARDS MY SPIRITUAL WELLNESS AND HEALING

1. _____
   _____
   _____
   _____

2. _____
   _____
   _____
   _____

3. _____
   _____
   _____
   _____

JOURNAL & NOTES

_____

_____

_____

_____

_____

_____

_____

_____

_____

_____

_____

_____

_____

_____

_____

THANK YOU

I thank God and the Universe for choosing me for such a meaningful life mission. I thank my dear family in heaven, Mom, Dad, Cliff, Stewart and Sean. I am so very grateful and thankful that God blessed me to have you for the time that I did. I thank my oldest daughter, Ashley. You are an amazing woman! I love you. Thank you to my youngest daughter Kennedy, you truly are an inspiration! I love you. You are going to do amazing things! Always allow your special light to shine in this world! To Brandon, thank you. Thank you to my dear aunt, the late Julia Pate, I thank you for years of love and support. I miss you dearly. Thank you to my Aunt Jannette for your love, support, thoughtfulness and laughter. To Aunt Francis, thank you for your love and support. To Uncle Wesley, thank you. To Sharon, Terrence, Brandy, Tank, Kalel and Greg I love you guys. To Sedera, love you! To my cousins, thank you and I love you all. To Tanya, Gary, Carl, Sharee, Kim, Loretta and Doris, I am so blessed to have you in my life, love you. To Jana and Evvy, thank you for your love, support and bringing people together, love you guys. To Jasmine, Courtney, Darius, Union and Jeaniyah I love y'all to pieces! To all of my nieces and nephews, God children and stepchildren; you are all destined for greatness! Thank you to Dr. Daniel Williams; thank you for giving me nuggets of wisdom that I will carry with me forever. Thank you to Adele Forster, who is one of the greatest mentors that a woman could have! To Tara, thank you for years of love, support, encouragement and sisterhood. Love You! Hey Tiff! Love you bunches. To Pat, thank you for a lifetime of love, support, friendship and sisterhood. To mugs, thank you for years of friendship, love you! To Karl and Howard great friends last a lifetime. To Angela, thank you for being a dear friend. To Carol, Debra, Lisa, Latoya and Tamika, love you guys! To Shameeka thank you for being a friend and inspiration! To Sabrina M, Thank you for my first Fierce Cut. To Sabrina lovejoy, Love you Sis!

To Tracey in Brooklyn, love you sis! To Teka, thank you for helping me to keep my hair together. To Pat Morton, thank you for wonderful memories that make me smile. To the SSA crew, I love and miss y'all! To the Snyder High crew, love you guys. To all of the nurses and receptionists at the children's infusion Center at Egleston Children's Hospital, thank you for all that you do! To Dr.lee, thank you for being an amazing principle to Kennedy and for all your love and support! To Chattahoochee Elementary School, thank you for your love and support! Love you guys!

To all the voters and protestors, thank you for being World Changers!